PURCHASE PLANNING GUIDE FOR LIGHTING SYSTEMS

It is not the beauty of a building you should look at; it's the construction of the foundation that will stand the test of time.

–David Allan Coe

Construction of Institute is like a game of Chess; you win only when you choose your weapons right.

–Abhinav Bharadwaj

PURCHASE PLANNING GUIDE FOR LIGHTING SYSTEMS

ANUBHAV JAIN

Worldwide Publishing by

PENDOWN PRESS
Powered by **Gullybaba Publishing House Pvt. Ltd.,**
An ISO 9001 & ISO 14001 Certified Co.,
Regd. Office: 2525/193, 1st Floor, Onkar Nagar-A, Tri Nagar,
Delhi-110035
Ph.: 09350849407, 09312235086
E-mail: info@pendownpress.com
Branch Office: 1A/2A, 20, Hari Sadan, Ansari Road,
Daryaganj, New Delhi-110002
Ph.: 011-45794768
Website: PendownPress.com

First Edition: 2020
Price: ₹259/-
ISBN: 978-93-89601-30-5

Layout and Cover Designed by Pendown Graphics Team
Printed and Bound in India by Thomson Press India Ltd.

Contents

About the Author

Anubhav Jain is the director at his family-owned business of lights by the name of Jainsons Lights Pvt. Ltd. established in 1975. He has experience in the lighting industry of over 10 years as he started working in the family business after his graduation in business administration. Soon after joining the business he quickly realised that the lighting field has a lot of technical aspects and thus educated himself on the field of lighting technology and effective lighting design. Till now, he and his team have guided the promoters and design consultants on numerous projects. With the launch of LED lights Anubhav help setup the company their domestic production capabilities so that the company can offer great quality product and customised lighting solution to its customers. The lighting industry in the wake of huge competition and lack of customer awareness is going through its darkest phase ever. The acceptable and commonly available product quality has fallen considerably and unaware customers are purchasing the substandard product. LED light technology can offer huge energy efficiency and long product life which the customer is not able to utilise and getting mislead. This has hugely disturbed the author thus he has started a mission of customer awareness.

This book is a huge step in this mission and also covers many other topics like ways to design effective lighting solution and latest trends in the lighting industry. The author also wishes to educate the interior& designers and construction design and consulting fertility on the ways of effective lighting design and thus enable them to offer a better lighting solution to their clients.

1

INTRODUCTION

I am a certified lighting designer and involved in designing and selling lighting products for over a decade. My company Jainsons Lights Pvt. Ltd. is one of the most trusted names in the lighting industry since 1975 and our team holds a cumulative experience of over 100 years. The team includes my father Mr. Rajan Jain who has started the business and has a huge experience in fancy light manufacturing. My brother Madhur Jain is a certified lighting designer from Sydney university.

This book is a cumulative result of knowledge of these people and other experienced people in our team.Primarily we are sellers of lighting products and solutions but have a very conventional approach to it. We believe in selling the right lighting solution to the customer as per their requirement rather than just force-feeding them what is in stock or what he is being wrongly specifiedalready. We have worked on over 500 successful projects and got huge benefits to our clients with the effective lighting design we created there. Whenever a lighting plan is more optimised and designed to suit the customer needs, chances are it optimizes the cost of the project too. Thus, for the lighting sellers, this may seem counterproductive, but we as a company, have a far-sighted approach to benefit the customer and getting more repeat businessis the objective of this exercise.

On the contrary, we can see a lot of unethical business practices being followed in the industry. A new design or feature of light is promoted for its uniqueness and aesthetics without checking its utility to the customer. That is sometimes in the wake of using the latest technology or design of the product, the basic utility, customer's requirement and other factors like maintenance and life of the product are compromised. Their intention is also to suggest a unique design and over charge a customer as he cannot compare prices in the market for the same easily.

Through this book we also want to address huge problems in the lighting industry. The technology is such that it's fast-evolving and customers are little aware of it. So, the industry in the pressure of competition, is moving towards a very low-quality standards with product life of 1-2 years. This is true with even big old companies and big so-called brands too. I mentioned so-called for the reason that some brands are built by balloon marketing within a very short period and may not have that technical know-how and experience in the market a big company should have. This often confuses customers and they associate quality and reliability to these brands. This brings competition pressure on the well-established players and they have to bring down their quality to sustain themselves in the market.

Although most customers are quality conscious and they are looking for the best quality product and the best solution for them, they are hugely clouded by all this. When wrong practice becomes an industry norm, then the law of majority takes over. That is if the majority is even with something wrong, for the outsiderit becomes the right thing because common sense goes with the majority.

My objective to write this book is to educate the end consumers, lighting professionals, interior designers and architects about the common ill practices in the lighting industry and suggest them the ways in which they can take a very well-informed purchase decision. I will tell them factors to look for while auditing the quality of lighting system and how to select the best vendor for themselves. They will also be able to understand the basic principles of lighting design and the latest trends in lighting design which will help them design effective lighting design for themselves and their customers.

I wish this book to be the harbinger of a positive change in the troubled and dying lighting industry and all the stakeholders of the industry can benefit from the book.

CHALLENGES IN LED LIGHT TECHNOLOGY AND USE

LED light technology and what customers should know and check before purchasing

LED stands for light emitting diode and is the latest technology in lighting industry. It is still very fast developing and as a technology, it is such that continuous development/ improvement is always going on. Moreover, there is no standard product, lamp or type of fixture. Thus, customer awareness is a key while making the purchase decision.There are so many nuances in the product that any layman may take a wrong purchase decision if he/she is misguided.

1. Types of LED and their application

There are many types of LED Chips that are produced ideally for different type of applications and have different advantages/features.

1.1 Low power SMD LED: These LEDs are up to 5 watt each chip and they generally need a special PCB (printed circuit board) to be mounted on and to provide them power to.

These LEDs being low power are generally used in clusters and are thus good for diffused spread lighting. That is, it is good for areas where we need ambient and general lighting.

They have the advantage of better heat management and better lumen efficiency. That is, we need to invest less in the housing or the body of the light fitting with these LED and thus they are more cost effective. They, being a lower wattage Led chip and the easy heat management with them, helps achieve a high lumen per watt output and high lumen per rupee spend output. In simple words for each rupee spent and each wattage of energy we can get higher light output from these LEDs that is when the product designer wants. Meaning technology-wise the SMD LEDs have this advantage but if the product is ill designed, then these advantages can be compromised to any extent. Thus, be mindful of the product design too, which I will mention later in the book. These LEDs are used in tube lights, LED bulbs, LED panels etc.

SMDLED have a LED chip packed in a body covered by layer of Phosphorus to provide the desired colour

1.2 High power COB LEDs: These are chips on board LED and as the name suggests they have a cluster of many small LED chips mounted on a single board. They don't require a PCB to power them, due to dense concentration of LED chips, they have in a small area. We required better heat management with these chips. They are used for directional lighting as the small single light emitting areas makes easy to give direction with the use of right optics.

In a COB LED, multiple chips are packaged on a PCB powered directly.

Their main applications are in places like retail showrooms for product lighting and accent lighting in homes.

Hence, while purchasing and for planning light scheme, we can select the suitable fixture and suitable type of above LED to create a better optimum balance between cost and utility.

SMD LED lights for focus lighting will not give the right light effect and thus will be less effective in achieving the objective of the lighting scheme, while using COB LED light fixture for ambient lighting can be costly and can create glare.

2. LED Driver and Purchasing Decisions

LED runs on constant low voltage DC current. Thus we need Ac-Dc converters to get the desired current required to run an LED. If an LED chip is the heart of a product, A ballast or converter is the mind of an LED product. The life and quality of the LED product depends very much on the quality of the driver. So before buying an LED product, check the following features in a driver.

2.1 Isolated or non-isolated: Isolated drivers have a protection against high input voltage. Thus, they give a protection against LED damage due to high voltage, while non-isolated drivers are cost effective but can damage the LED. Wherever possible use an isolated driver which comes with many more other benefits too over non-isolated drivers.

2.2 Input voltage range: Indian voltage conditions are very rough and advisable voltage range of 100-300 volts is good for Indian conditions. Having an over input voltage protection is also advisable for extra protection. This means 100-300 is a range in which driver would keep running while over 300 if a driver has over voltage protection, it would go into protection mode and shut the driver off to safeguard the driver from damage. For outdoor this protection can go up to 440 volts also.

2.3 Surge protection: Surge is a voltage fluctuation that occur in millisecond and can damage the driver. This is how lights and other electronics items get damaged when generators are switched on as the generator produces huge amount of continuous surge. For indoor a surge protection of 2kv and above is advisable and for outdoor a minimum of 4kv surge protection is required.

2.4 Power factor: This is a ratio between the energy consumption and the current that a product withdraws from the grid. This means if the power factor of any product is less than 90, it means that it withdraws more current from the grid it should do ideally. The electricity distribution companies measure this and will put a multiplier on your electricity bill for this. Thus, if your LED lights have low power factor, then you will get a higher electricity bill. A power factor of above 0.9 is considered good.

2.5 Efficiency: This means how much energy is used up by the LED ballast to drive the LED. That is if the LED is of 10 w and the total power consumption by the ballast is 12 w, this means 10 divided by 12 the efficiency of the ballast is 83 percent. Thus, higher is the efficiency, better it is, as less electricity is consumed. An efficiency of above 85 percent is considered good.

2.6 Total harmonic distortion: The sum of total harmonic distortions created by the ballast is termed as total harmonic distortion or commonly known as THD. These interferences disturb other electronics devices like mobiles, computers televisions. Generally, a THD (total harmonic distortion) level less than 15 percent is considered good.

3. LED chips

A LED chip is the heart of any LED lights, as they are the ones that give the actual light. The most innovation happens in LED chips only. Manufacturing a good quality LED chip involves huge R&D, years of experience and huge manufacturing set up, thus selecting the right LED is hugely critical for the success of a lighting setup. We need to consider the following factors for selecting the right LED.

3.1 Brand of the LED: There are many premium huge brands of LED manufacturers that have a reputation in the market for their quality due to their experience and brilliant manufacturing facilities and superb quality standards they maintain. Let me mention some popular brands in LED chips which are a good combination of price and quality in the market. And also, different companies are specialist in different types of LED, thus we need to look out for that. It is highly advisable to use such LEDs that are popular and already being widely used in the market. Below mentioned is a selection guide for the brands according to LED type.

COB LED – Cree, Lumileds (which is a Phillips company). Bridgelux, Samsung, Citizen,

SMD LED – Everlight, Bridgelux, Osram, Edison

3.2 Lumen output : Lumen is the unit of light output and in LED light industry there is no standard of lumen per watt. That is every LED chip manufacturer have their own specifications of how much lumen per watt they are going to provide. Then each brand has many ranges of LED with different lumen per watt options. They have economical range with low lumen efficacy that is per watt lumen and premium ranges with high efficacy also. Thus, it is the final product manufacturer whose role is most crucial here. It is simply because it is he who decides as to which LED should be selected in his products.

Hence, always ask manufacturers to mention lumen level in the product and brand of led chip used in their product. It also depends on the design of the product how much total final lumen output the product is going to emit, thus do ask the manufacture to specify that number too.

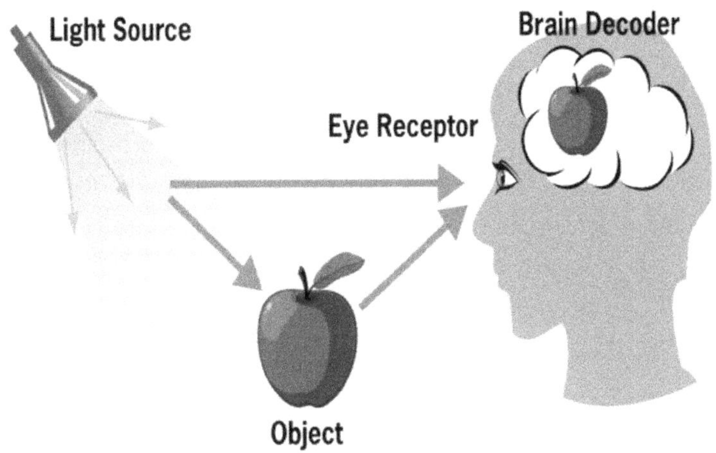

3.3 CRI: In simple terms, this is the quality of the light output of an LED which will bring out the accuracy of colour's shade and contrast in the item displayed in that light. Thus, if the CRI is low the item will look less appealing and beautiful while higher CRI LED will bring out the true beauty in the interior or products lit by it. This has a huge application in retail, home and hospitality. Your purchasing decision should include considering this factor. A CRI of above 80 in warm white/neutral white and above 70 in cool white is the minimum industry standard below which you should not accept. But for better results and specially in some special applications like retail a CRI of over 90 is preferred.

3.4 Driving current of the LED: All the LED chips have a range of wattage in which it can be run. So, if the LED will be operated at the minimum specified wattage, it will provide higher lumen efficacy, lower colour shift and will have a longer running life. Similarly, it is vice versa if LED is operated at the maximum wattage. Hence, it is always advisable for customers to ask the manufacturer the LED model used in the final product and ask what is the operating wattage of each LED. The user should prefer that LED to be run at the minimum power only.

3.5 Colour of LED: LED light technology does not have any standard colour of light as it was in other previous technologies of lights. Though the most prevalent ones are cool white (6000k), warm white(3000k) and neutral white(4000k) , in LED chips, there are numerous shades available from the range of 2200k to 7500k; that is orange to bluish white. So now designers have an option to choose many different colours in their lighting layout. They can choose 2700 k for warmer look in hospitality applications or use a 7500k to enhance the look of diamond jewelry in retail showrooms.

This brings another challenge for the manufacturer and consumer to maintain the colour consistency in the product. Thus, this is a major factor, while purchasing which needs to be considered.

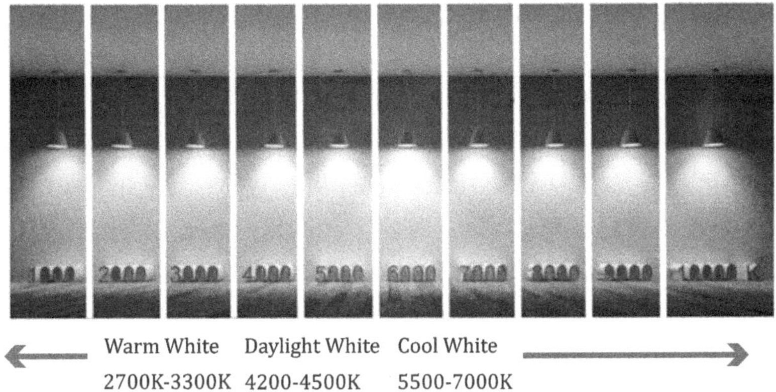

3.6 Material of LED Chips: LED chips are made with different materials which define the quality of the chip. A SMD LED package can be made of plastic, ceramic or any other material. Some materials like plastic are not specified for outdoor use, thus be wary of that fact as due to market price competition pressures, such misuse is prevalent in the market.

4. Housing of LED lights

This is the case or the body used to manufacture a LED light. It is a very important factor and has to be considered before purchase of light.

4.1 Material of the body: This is the material of which housing of a LED light is made of. LED has a special requirement as mentioned earlier to manage the heat produced as a by- product. Thus, most widely used product is aluminum that is a good mix between price and heat conductivity. Nowadays other cheaper materials like plastic is also prevalent due to competition in the market. Thus, being a customer be wary of the materials of the body of the LED light product. Cheaper mass scale standard products like tube lights and bulbs can be in plastic. Other products like spotlight and downlight panel should be in metal aluminum housing only. SMD low power LED up to 0.2w when operated at a lower than minimum wattage can be used with plastic body. This is also only if we are using a metal core PCB. And in most conditions, the life of plastic LED light products will be shorter than the ones made of aluminum. Hence, while purchasing lights make sure to check what is the material of the product.

Many manufacturers also mention a working ambient temperature that is often quite low as a form of disclaimer.

5. Optics and diffuser

Any diffuser, reflectors, lenses or any other kind of optics has an impact on the efficacy of the complete fixture that is the amount of light coming out of the LED chips and the amount of actually usable light may be different due to wastage of lights because of all the optics mentioned above. Thus, the quality of these materials matters a lot.

5.1 Reflectors and lenses: Optics like Reflectors and lenses are used in focused lighting with COB LED chips generally. They come in various beam angles. The amount of light that will spread or be focused will depend on the degree of the beam angle.The higher is the beam angle of the reflector, more the light will spread. Thus, it is critical to select the right beam angle suitable to your lighting layout.

Moreover, better the quality of the reflector and lens, better the light output and a more even distribution of light. In the common practice, there are two types of reflector/ lens, branded and unbranded. Branded reflector/lens have higher efficiency, and are of good quality and obviously more expensive vice versa for the non-branded reflector/ lens., Hence, if you need a good quality product, go for branded reflector/lens and if a lower price is the preference, you can select local reflector/lens for your products.

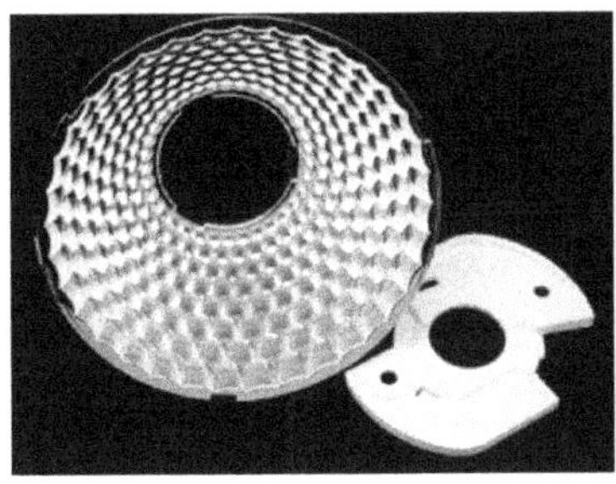

5.2 Diffusers: When we use SMD lights in indoor application, reducing glare and improvingand improving aesthetics are important. Thus, diffusers are used for dispersing the light so that multiple LEDs are not visible. Again, higher the efficiency of diffuser better is the light efficacy that is more usable light coming out of the fitting. So, consumers need to be aware of this fact and select a product with branded diffusers only.

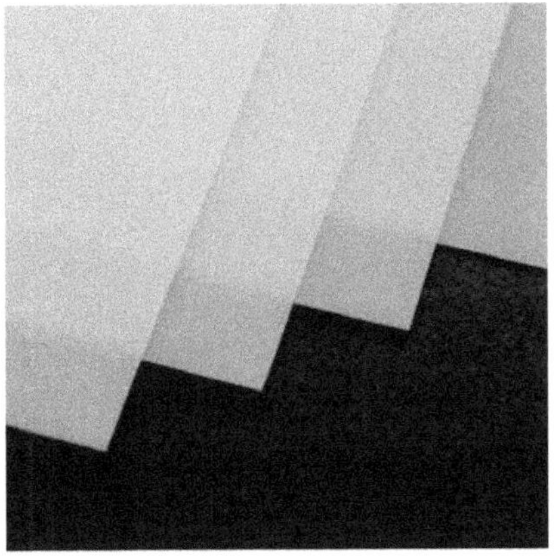

6. PCB

As mentioned above, many low power SMD and high-power LED need an electrical board to power the LED. This has electrical circuits that wire the LED in correct series and parallel combination. Thus, the LED can be run at the desired current of the available ballast. Generally, a metal core PCB is used for LED but due to current price competitions and pressures in the market other materials like FR-4 (composite material composed of woven fiberglass cloth with an epoxy resin binder that is flame resistant) or not metal non heat conducting materials are also used. These are not advisable and unless LED is run at a lower wattage than their specified minimum wattage, these are not good for the LED chips. In metal core PCB also, there are many qualities available. So higher the wattage of the product, better quality of PCB should be used.

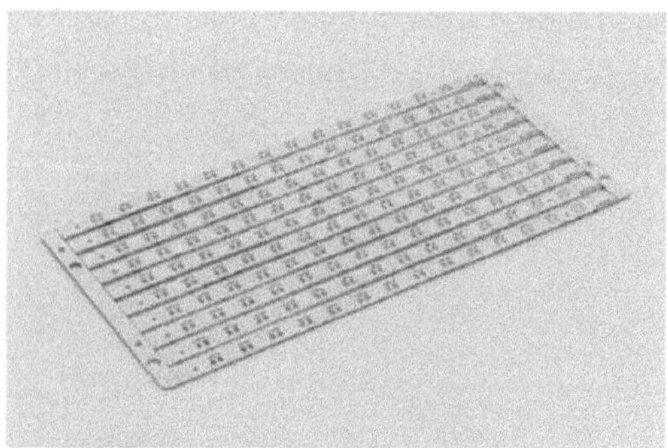

3

CHOICE OF VENDOR

How to select the right vendor for your lighting requirement?

There are two types of products that are available in the market. One is the products sold by big companies sold under their brand name, most such brands have OEM factories that manufacture the product for them. Other are the products that are assembled by not so big companies but can be customised as per your requirement.

Purchasing only on the basis of the trust of the brand name is not advisable in any industry and it is more so not advisable in the lighting industry. The lighting industry as mentioned earlier has so much of technical aspects and total non-standardisation with many of its componentsas a whole. Thus Customer awareness of the product is critical. Following are the factors that you need to keep in mind before choosing the right vendor for you or which brand of product to choose.

1. Origin of products

This is a very important criterion and one should prefer products made in India. The components can be manufactured anywhere in the world but if the final product is also assembled out of India it will not be that reliable. Reason being, if the company is getting products manufactured abroad they have limited control over the quality of the product. Indian products are more suited to domestic conditions. A company may have different products with different origins, thus check for each product.

2. Guarantee terms, and service after guarantee

Check the guarantee year term and more importantly check for market feedback on how much company is true to their commitments. Gurantee term means the number of years of guarantee the company is giving on the products. Generally, guarantee term ranges from 1 to 5 years on the products. But the trickier part is to check how much the company is true to their after-sales commitments. Moreover, only guarantee period is not crucial, but capability and willingness to provide the maintenance services on the product after the guarantee is also important. That is to assume you have purchased a good quality product with a life of over 10 years, then you need to maintain your lighting setup after the guarantee period. Most big brands will not provide you with this maintenance service. A practical scenario is that the designs of the products change frequently in the industry and most companies work on use and throw model to get more sales with replacements. But this is a very rough deal for customers. If let say 10 per cent of the lights in a set up get faulty after guarantee and the same design not available with the company and they are not providing any repair services. In this case the customer is stuck or then the whole setup has to be replaced. So, this a huge factor to be considered before purchasing the lights.

3. The financial strength of the company

Lighting business had gone through a lot of challenges lately. The industry shifted to LED, the LED technology is so fast developing, that it is a challenge in itself. There have been many irregularities in the market where companies misquoted in some government (EESL) tenders. To win the tenders they quoted too aggressively, some provided material in losses, some provided substandard product which later failed in the market that resulted in huge amount of money being stuck in payments. Moreover, price wars between these players led to huge losses due to which many big companies in the lighting industry are unstable and few also went insolvent. Thus, if you by mistake purchase product from an unstable company and later the company faces financial troubles, you are not going to get any service on your product. Thus, please check the financial strength of the company before investing your money with them.

4. Customer portfolio

The industry is so vast and technically diverse, it is mostly common that companies have expertise in a particular type or application of lights. If your application is specialised, then check the customer portfolio of the company to verify that you have chosen the right company for your requirement.

5. Goodwill of the company

This is a major factor not to be confused with the popularity of the brand. Today's world is of marketing and brand popularity can be built in a short span with huge marketing budgets. While goodwill is based on years of customer experience and market feedback. Thus, check from the reviews and experiences of the recent customer experiences, of the company or a brand. The LED light industry has now become a consumer services industry like other consumer electronics and appliances industry. Hence, this is a major factor you should consider. Select a company that has a minimum of 10 years of experience in the industry and out of them who's market feedback for their after sales service is excellent.

EFFECTIVE LIGHTING DESIGN

A good and an effective lighting layout plays an important role in enhancing any space and is critical for bringing out the true beauty of the interior design. A well-designed effective lighting design helps to boost sales by increasing the conversion ratein the retail showrooms. In factories and offices, it helps boost work productivity. In homes, it creates a lively warm feeling which uplifts the mood. In hotel and restaurants, it helps in enhancing the customer experience by creating the right ambience.

Hence, you should find a lighting expert who can guide you regarding effective lighting design and layout while planning and executing any project. I will provide here what should all be covered and taken care of while you are planning lights for any space.

1. Defining the objectives

Understanding the requirement of the lighting layout is very important. This is like laying out the foundation of the lighting design by understanding the objective the lighting has to achieve. If this is mapped out clearly, then only better planning is possible. We need to figure out all the possible uses of the space and plan for lighting requirement according to those uses.

2. Layer of lighting

Primarily, there are three layers of lighting that decide which type of lighting layout will suit a place and which kind of fixtures to be used. These are namely ambient, task and accent lighting. The general light required in a space that is the basic amount of light required is called the ambient lighting. Task lighting, as the name suggests, is the light required to achieve a particular task or activity to be carried out in the space. The lighting that is used to enhance the aesthetics of a space or highlight any design features is called the accent lighting. So, any lighting consultant or interior designer needs to map out the requirement of light in these categories and create a proper balance between them. After which finally planning for the lighting layout can be started.

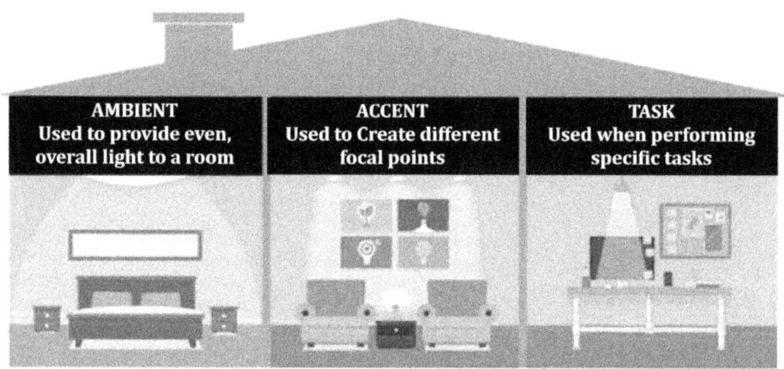

3. The requirement of light levels

Now the designer has to decide how much light level is required. For this, there is an easily available standard guide designer can refer to, which gives the suggested light levels for a different kind of space and task. A designer with the help of this guide in consideration with other factors can decide on a suitable light level for any space.

4. Colour of light

Different applications require the different colours of light to be chosen keeping the preference of the customer, that is the user, also in mind. And there are again some common guidelines available on the basis of science which designers can follow. For example, a warmer colour is preferred in bedroom to help people relax and sleep better like the mobiles have night mode these days. This is because white light disturbs sleep at night as per studies. Similarly, lot of similar guidelines are available and should be followed. Nowadays colour tunable lights are also available with which user can simply switch the colour of light with the help of simple controls.

5. CRI of light

In simple terms, Colour Rendering Index (CRI) means the ability of the light to depict accuracy of colour's shades and contrast in the object it is illuminating. Thus, higher the CRI better it is for the user. Some applications like product lighting in retail require this a lot, hence using a LED of above 90 CRI in such applications is advisable.

6. Electrical layout

If a lighting designer needs full freedom in designing the light layout, then it should be made sure that the right planning is done for the electrical layout so the lights can be placed and powered accordingly. Availability of wiring connections and choice of switching is an integral part of the planning of lighting layout. Generally, wiring and electrical layout are decided much earlier than the lighting plan, thus integration and advance planning of lighting layout is required otherwise the designer will be limited by the available electrical layout.

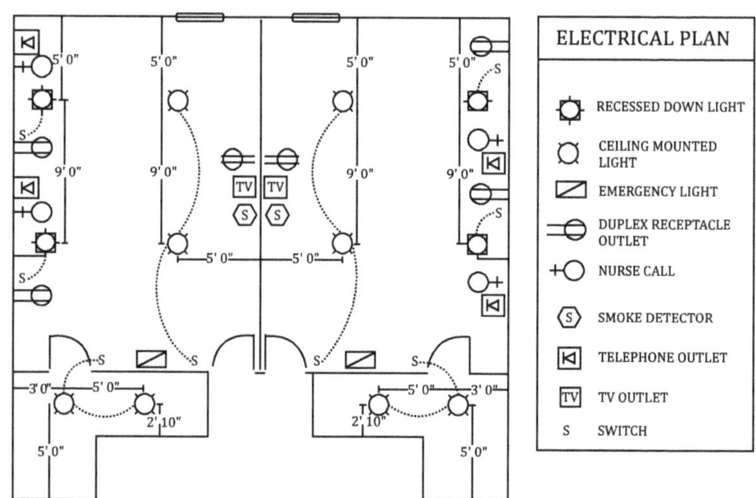

6. Selection of lighting fixtures

Designers also select the suitable light fixtures, the wattage of light, beam angle of light, suitable light source, etc.

7. Use of lighting design software

When the desired lighting level has been decided, then a

designer has to use a lighting design software to ascertain how many light fixtures are required of a particular wattage to achieve that amount of the light level. There is no mathematical or another way possible to ascertain this otherwise.

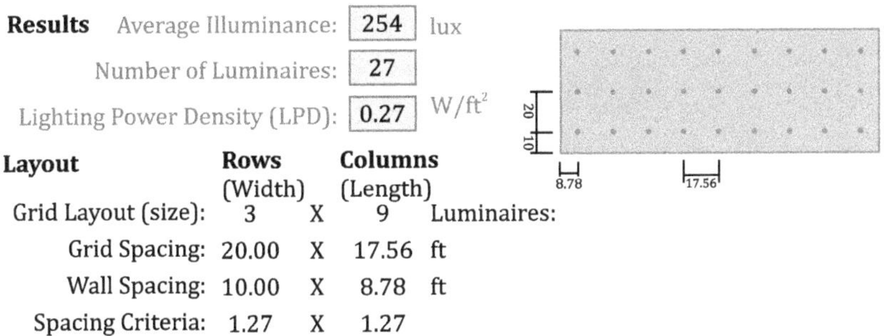

8. Incorporating lighting layout in the AutoCAD designs

After the lighting layout has been decided by the designer, it should be incorporated in the AutoCAD designs of the space so the whole designing and execution can be done in coordination with other experts.

LATEST TRENDS IN LIGHTING DESIGN

Over the years lighting technology and interior design trends have changed a lot with ongoing fast changing requirements of the users. Thus, the trends and norms of effective lighting design have also changed with time. Let's go over some of these latest trends.

1. Residential lighting

Interior design trends in residential sector has revolutionised over the years. Customers require the latest designs and technology to be used at their home to achieve maximum comfort and aesthetics.

Most common practice in the residential interior design these days is to have a false ceiling. This is a major fundamental change in the concept of residential interiors and most widely used. Thus, the role of concealed false ceiling lights that are installed by cutting a hole in the false ceiling is very prevalent. Also cove lighting is thus widely used too. ALED flexible strip lighting is used for cove lighting which can come in various colours and types. With the many requirements that are fulfilled with these concealed false ceiling light nowadays that the role of tube lights and decorative lights have become limited. Decorative lights only now are used for enhancing the aesthetics and thus have become like a means of interior decoration. Tube lights are considered least preferred way of providing ambient lighting in the room. This I am mentioning with a perspective of urban modern homes. The use of tube lights and LED lamps are still most prevalent if we look at the whole industry and the country as a whole. But as we are talking about lighting design I will limit to the application and scenario in urban modern requirement where lighting design is required mostly.

2. Retail showroom lights

In the world of aggressive marketing and business competition, each and every aspect of product selling and display is very important for the business success. Retail lighting has some basic principles that a retailer must keep in mind before planning for the lighting of their showroom which are given below:

2.1 Defining the objective of retail lighting: A retailer should be aware and have clarity on the objectives of retail of lightingretail lighting which are often forgotten during the construction process. The retailers sometimes forget their objective of the whole showroom of maximum sales and focus more on just aesthetic appeal of the store which hold limited importance in boosting sales. The true objective of retail lighting are as follows:

- Entice customers in store, further attract them to right corners and create an engaging atmosphere.

- The product should be the star and should stand out of anything in the store.
- Light should bring out the true beauty of the product helping the customer to evaluate the merchandise and make a quick purchase.

  These are the objectives of retail lighting and now let's discuss how the below mentioned new trends help achieve them.

2.2 Contrast lighting: This is the latest trend in retail lighting or product display lighting. Traditionally in the retail showroom, it was considered that well-lit showroom is good for the showroom and it enhances the outlook of the showroom. While the prudent thinking to this is if you have uniform lighting all across the showroom, then nothing stands out. On the other hand, if you have more light on the products rather than empty spaces this helps create an engaging atmosphere where customers are drawn to the product. The suggested ratio between light levels of product and empty spaces is 10:1 minimum, going up to 20:1. That is for an effective contrast lighting; make sure to have at least 10 times more light levels on the product rather than empty spaces.

Retail showroom with uniform lighting where nothing stands out

Retail showroom with contrast lighting which makes the product in a store stand out

2.3 Colour and CRI of the light: Led colour and its quality hold huge importance in the effectiveness of the product display. The color shade, spectrum of the light and CRI are major factors as they can majorly influence the outlook of the product and in turn affect sales. Warmer light colour shades (in layman terms yellowish light) have more content of red ,yellow and similar colour light in their spectrum thus they are good for lighting such colour products. And vice versa the cooler light colour shades (in layman terms white light) have more content of blues, greens and similar colour shades thus are good for lighting similar colour products. Another important factor is the CRI of the light that is the Colour Rendering Index of the light. This means that the visible accuracy of colour's shade and contrast of any product depends upon the CRI of the light it is viewed in. In simple terms, the higher the CRI of the light being used will result in a higher accuracy of colour shade and contrast of the product.

Low CRI makes the product look less appealing to the customers

High CRI led makes the look of the merchandise more appealing to the customers by bringing out the true beauty of the product

A higher CRI light enhances the outlook of the product and thus helps in better sales conversion, thus always a higher CRI light should be used in retail showrooms. To simplify, I would like to mention some simple suggestions regarding this matter:

Suggested use of light colour and CRI

Type of Application	Colour of light	CRI of light
Women clothing and fashion	3000k (Warm white)	90 CRI
Men clothing and fashion	4000k (Natural white)	90 CRI
Gold and colour stone jewelry	3000k (Warm white)	90 CRI
Diamond jewelry	6500/7500 k	
Electronics and appliances	3000k (Warm white)	90 CRI

Legend

Code	Generic Name	Description
3k(3000k)	Warm White	Colour shade close to an incandescent lamp.
6k(6000k)/ 65k(6500k)	Cool white	colour similar to pure white light.
4k (4000k)	Natural white	Colour shade between 3k and 6k like milky moon light
75k (7500k)		Special LED which has bluish white tone.

3. Tunable & Dimmable Lights

Another latest innovation in the lighting industry has been the development of tunable and dimmable lights. In simple terms, these lights have a function where you can adjust the colour temperature that is the colour of the light from 3000k (warm white) to 6500k(cool white). Moreover, you can also dim the light from 100 to 1 per cent. These are controlled wirelessly; thus, no setup is required and thus these are also a very smart system. You can group the lights together and operate them in whatever way you like. Prefixed scenes can be created and schedules can be set. There are various uses of this technology in various applications and areas . In homes, this gives the user flexibility and comfort of choosing any colour of light and any light level. This is very useful as it is a proven fact that the colour of light affects human behavior. Cool light makes you more active and warm yellow light helps you relax and is a recreational light. Thus, this system gives more flexibility to the customer. In retail showrooms also, this has a huge application. Many a time we have different products in one retail showroom that are better displayed in different colours of light. For example, in jewelry showroom, white light is needed for diamond & silver jewelry, while yellow warm light is best for coloured stones and gold jewelry.

Tunable systems are wirelessly controlled with a remote control or mobile apps.

4. Track lighting systems

This is a flexible system of lighting where we have a channel which has running power throughout its length, which means that any compatible light can be clipped on anywhere along the length of the track. Thus, this provides the flexibility to the customer to have the light focused on the area where he wants. This system has a huge application in the retail industry as the light layout can be altered as per the change in the product display.

Another advantage of this system is that it is much easier to maintain and upgrade the lights. For example, in false ceiling light if you need to replace or upgrade the light you need a suitable light that matches the cut size in the ceiling. Thus, wherever possible, use the track lighting system to avail all these advantages.

5. Strip and Linear Aluminum Channel-Profile lighting

Strip lights are LED light on a flexible PCB. These can be cut at customisable length and run on standard constant voltage system which is easier to manage. These are used in many applications like for ceiling cove lighting and mostly accent purposes. Nowadays, a new system of linear aluminum profile system has been developed with the help of which flexible strip light system is used for various applications. The profile lighting system uses an aluminum section as the body of the light and has a diffuser to diffuse the light installed. These are widely used for their aesthetic looks and sleek designs. The various applications in which these profile lights are used are as follows:

- Office desk lighting
- Showcase lighting
- Wardrobe lighting
- Cabinet lighting
- Step lights
- Countertop lights in the kitchens
- Used to create lighted shelves
- Showroom display shelf lighting
- Floor embedded lights

CONCLUSION

To summarise, I would like to say that lighting plays a major role in the life of everyone. It has a huge impact on the quality of life and success of any venture. Moreover, the field has a lot of technical aspects and due to Indian conditions and market competitions, there are many ill practices that are prevalent in the market which lead to a huge disservice to the consumers. Also design professionals are also not able to design effective lighting solutions for the consumers due to these factors. Designers know that right lighting is the most crucial factor for the success of their project and they are always looking for someone to guide them so that they can get the lighting of the project right. My mission is to educate the lighting professionals and design fertility for effective lighting. Thus, the whole industry and end consumers are benefited at large.

To help this cause if any individual needs any help regarding anything in the lighting industry they are most welcome to meet me and I would try to help to the fullest of my capabilities.

Reach my team to book an appointment with me at our showroom.

 website -www.jainsonslights.com

 Corporate no. 9266629996

www.ingramcontent.com/pod-product-compliance
Ingram Content Group UK Ltd.
Pitfield, Milton Keynes, MK11 3LW, UK
UKHW062256290726
14090UKWH00017B/731

9 789389 601305